Bears

If you walk on a crack,

2

a bear will put you in a sack.

3

If you step on a stone,

a bear will pinch your ankle bone.

If you walk under the trees,

a bear will shoot you with some peas.

And if you rest
on Big Bear Street,
the bears will surely
tickle your feet.